SAKURA

Joseph R. Adomavicia

JOSEPH R. ADOMAVICIA

"Sakura"

Written and arranged by Joseph R. Adomavicia

All Rights Reserved.

SAKURA

CONTENTS

Section I: Senryu

12. Arms of a Crimson Sunset
13. Ocean of Grief
14. Keen Eyes
15. Hope is Alive
16. These Ears
17. Meditative State
18. These Hands
19. These Feet
20. Wake up
21. These Demons
22. It Is More Than Empty Rooms
23. Black Roses
24. These Words
25. The Stain Remains
26. Eye of the Beholder
27. These Ghosts
28. Carry On
29. These Days
30. I Care

31. I Didn't Take the Whole Day Off
32. Flies
33. Love Over Hate
34. Men and Women
35. Cut and Burn Carefully
36. Self-Worth
37. Self-Reflection
38. Regret is a Killer
39. Boots
40. Vices
41. Planting Thoughts
42. Remain Brave
43. In That Order
44. Unforgiven
45. Into Tomorrow
46. Stoneless Graves
47. Your Own Power
48. Searching for a Home
49. Crumpling
50. Bets
51. Horror Comes in the Day Too
52. Swing
53. Passenger

54. Stuck in the Breeze
55. End Game
56. Reflections
57. Remedy
58. Believe It
59. This Disease
60. This Calling
61. Heart of Stone
62. Manifestation
63. Home
64. Why Crush One, When There Are Many?
65. Standing Tall
66. This Truth
67. Finders Keepers
68. The Motto
69. Not Your Average Piercing
70. Hypocrite
71. Perks
72. Write On
73. Peiskos
74. This Dance
75. Guidance

Section 2: Haiku

77. The Seasons Get Along
78. We Wake Again
79. Under the Sun
80. On the Wings of Truth
81. Watching Waterfalls
82. Stalker
83. Listen Closely
84. Light Will Shine Through
85. Bloody Waters
86. Cleansing
87. The Night Tide
88. Space Cadet
89. Web Weaving
90. A Sweet Summer Day
91. A Day at the Beach

Section 3: Tanka

93. Safe Spots
94. Acceptance
95. Sunset
96. Summertime

97. Be Happy
98. Faces in the Glass
99. Unlocking the Cage
100. In My Head
101. Our Universe
102. Ease My Senses
103. Know Your Path Too
104. Be Calm
105. Sweet Spots
106. My Inspiration
107. You Found My Light
108. Sanctuary
109. White Flag
110. Potency
111. Where is Home Now?
112. Bittersweet
113. There is an End
114. My Time of the Year
115. Is It In You?
116. It's Our Choices
117. I've Ignited
118. G Zero Zero (G00)
119. Memorial Day

Section 4: Choka

121. Advice From an Old Friend
123. Sakura
124. Stage Left

SAKURA

Edited by Joseph R. Adomavicia

Graphic Design by Mitch Green of RadPress Publishing

JOSEPH R. ADOMAVICIA

READER'S REFERENCE GUIDE

Senryu- Similar to a haiku, a senryu is a 3-lined Japanese-style poem consisting of the syllable count of 17 in the order of 5-7-5 and does not have to rhyme. Senryu are written in the context of ironies of life and life in general.

Haiku- A haiku is a 3-lined Japanese-style poem consisting of the syllable count of 17 in the order of 5-7-5. Haiku are written with the intent of depicting seasonal imagery and images of the world.

Tanka- A tanka is a 5-lined Japanese-style poem consisting of the syllable count of 31 syllables in the order of 5-7-5-7-7. Tanka poems encompass a thought or mood.

Choka- A Choka is a form of Japanese-style poetry that does not have a set amount of lines, but must end in an odd number of lines and is written in alternating lines of 5 and 7 syllables only ending with an extra line of 7 syllables. Choka poems are not required to rhyme.

SAKURA

SECTION I: SENRYU

JOSEPH R. ADOMAVICIA

<u>Arms of a Crimson Sunset</u>

Into the arms of
a crimson sunset I sail
Home away from home

SAKURA

<u>Ocean of Grief</u>

Tears just like raindrops

could form an ocean of grief

but who notices

Keen Eyes

Loud roars vultures soar
snakes slither insects crawl 'round
Keen eyes are needed

SAKURA

Hope is Alive
Cracks in concrete sprout
life in small doses serving
hope from a dark place

These Ears

These ears have heard lies
and with them and with time I've
learnt to see from them

Meditative State

Breathe inhale exhale

Like water on the seashore

Breathe inhale exhale

These Hands

These two hands work hard
through tough days oil-soaked cuts and
blood sweat and my tears

SAKURA

These Feet

Barefoot on glass shards

These two feet have walked for years

These feet will not fail

Wake Up

Wake up please wake up

Someone wake the nation and

care for more than self

SAKURA

These Demons

These demons have hold

Their grip is tight still I fight

for another day

JOSEPH R. ADOMAVICIA

It Is More Than Empty Rooms
Shine off hardwood floors
flood each room and broken blinds
hang from window sills

SAKURA

<u>Black Roses</u>

For you a bouquet

Black roses will have to do

Red just doesn't suit you

JOSEPH R. ADOMAVICIA

These Words
Are the foundation
and are the combination
of my life and strife

The Stain Remains

You can carve out the
heart of all the devil's deeds
but the stain remains

JOSEPH R. ADOMAVICIA

<u>Eye of the Beholder</u>

Clean thoughts dirty thoughts

both from the origin Eye

of the beholder

These Ghosts
They breed darkness and
hide light These ghosts have become
plight I will conquer

Carry On

Roars from the inside

Thunder rumbles from above

I will carry on

SAKURA

These Days
It is not about
one voice or one vote it is
the conglomerate

I Care

I care and still will

Part of my heart is for you

Even in my end

SAKURA

I Didn't Take the Whole Day Off

I wrote this today

A lone lazy senryu

This I wrote for you

Flies

Flies in mason jars

Trapped and buzzing without aim

Don't exert yourself

SAKURA

Love Over Hate

Love more than you hate

Hate will only decimate

Be better than that

Men and Women

Havoc on this earth

Spread by its men and women

We need more resolve

SAKURA

<u>Cut and Burn Carefully</u>

Scissors and a match

Cut the cord and burn the bridge

Spark a flame inside

Self-Worth

Prove your worth daily

To none other than yourself

Be your biggest fan

Self-Reflection

You don't know yourself
until you learn to reflect
on broad perspectives

Regret is a Killer

Don't forget the dream
you live each and every day
The regret will kill

SAKURA

<u>Boots</u>

Life is as it was

Plus or minus tolerance

Strap your boots on tight

Vices

Smoking or drinking

Seems like we all have vices

One up and one down

SAKURA

<u>Planting Thoughts</u>

Gather seeds of thought

Water them let them flourish

Repeat the cycle

Remain Brave

Stand tall with honor
even when gravity weighs
trudge on remain brave

SAKURA

In That Order

Anger grief relief

All feelings I'm glad I've felt

I can breathe again

Unforgiven

Fist to wall anger

Dismiss and bury her death

It was all her choice

Into Tomorrow

Phantom acoustics

sound like sorrow that moved on

into tomorrow

Stoneless Graves

A heavy burden

Helpless man displays dismay

For graves with no stones

SAKURA

Your Own Power

Life works in hard ways

Choose to live or fail to live

Feel your own power

Searching for a Home

Bury me in the
deep crevices of your heart
I will find my home

SAKURA

<u>Crumpling</u>

My troubled headspace

Pride crumples like dry paper

Bottle the remains

Bets

Stare into the sun

Hopefully the stars can heal

All bets on blindness

SAKURA

<u>Horror Comes in the Day Too</u>

Shipyard harmonics

Halloween horrors arrive

Silent screams by day

Swing

Swing around the truth

Salvage what's left of your lies

Your life to ruin

Passenger

Darkness lingering

Passenger of the cool night

Frail hands on shoulders

Stuck in the Breeze

Harsh bellows ring out

Sound waves bouncing off the trees

I'm stuck in the breeze

SAKURA

End Game

Sorrow is bitter

but the joy found at its end

is worth all the pain

Reflections

Mirror mirror fall

Shatter to pieces like me

Reflect on all things

<u>Remedy</u>

A worldwide cleansing

would not be the remedy

if afraid of change

Believe It
If given a chance
these lone wolf epiphanies
will change the world's views

SAKURA

<u>This Disease</u>

Have it as you will

This disease runs ocean deep

In my veins steeping

This Calling

I fear the far cries

Bringing forth only the truth

It's tough to embrace

SAKURA

<u>Heart of Stone</u>

This fire I admire

ignites creativity

from a heart of stone

<u>Manifestation</u>

Manifest courage

Harvest the will to succeed

and you will find you

Home

After all this time

home is still found in your arms

My life found solace

<u>Why Crush One, When There Are Many?</u>

A lone black hole soul

often relies on others

to brace their downfall

SAKURA

<u>Standing Tall</u>
Some towers crumble
Some towers stand vigilant
Will you stand or fall

This Truth

Naked truth runs wild

through the thick of day and night

You can't hide from it

SAKURA

<u>Finders Keepers</u>
Zero deductions
as you prove history true
What's found foul is vile

The Motto

Don't bite till bitten

that's always been the motto

Defensive offence

SAKURA

<u>Not Your Average Piercing</u>
A ray of sunlight
penetrates piercing through me
A squall of darkness

Hypocrite

Men in the mirror

My silver-tongued animates

Who am I today

SAKURA

<u>Perks</u>

Stand by me my love

Silence the noise silence made

Perks of a lone man

Write On

Write me intricate

Write me as the one who fell

I'll right my own path

SAKURA

Peiskos

Simple evening meal

Friends and family thankful

Soothing flames burn on

This Dance

My hands at your waist

We have this dance ardently

It's just you and I

SAKURA

Guidance

My biggest failures

have guided me to the truth

The fog dissipates

JOSEPH R. ADOMAVICIA

SECTION 2: HAIKU

SAKURA

The Seasons Get Along
The first bloom of Spring
has always welcomed in the
first days of Summer

We Wake Again

Life is like flowers

that bloom in early morning

We wake and flourish

SAKURA

Under the Sun

Flowers blowing by

under the care of sun rays

It hurts not helping

<u>On the Wings of Truth</u>

An invitation
I have offered in my words
My truth now in flight

On the wings of truth
my actions provide proof for
all my conviction

I will write until
both my hands seize ceasing to
write on anymore

Watching Waterfalls

Water cascading

I wish to fall with such grace

Giving back to life

Stalker

Time stalks like a creep

following you home at night

Run for your life's sake

Listen Closely

The sea's salty tang

Shells washed up on the seashore

Now listen closely

<u>Light Will Shine Through</u>

Draped in pure darkness

The night has crept into me

to bring out the light

SAKURA

Bloody Waters
Tender feet bled dry
walking shores like penny nails
Too late to return

Cleansing

Doused in kerosene

Burn all my shame to ashes

Heat of hellish fire

SAKURA

The Night Tide

What if I fade out

What if I swim the night tide

What if I fade out

Space Cadet

Ascend in orbit

Swim through galaxies of stars

Descend once again

Web Weaving

We weave webs where we
want Why wander wayward where
whirlwinds whip wildly

A Sweet Summer Day

Pink flowers blooming

Beauty relishing my life

Tranquility's grasp

Ah a sunflower

These righteous breaths of fresh air

Bright yellow and white

Cotton candy skies

Passion in a new disguise

Easing my mind's eye

Eyes on the skyline

All pink and blue through and through

A marvelous prize

A Day at the Beach

Calm waters glisten
My sunny day keeps shining
Dismissing gray days

Sand under my toes
Waves swishing on the seashore
Cool, calm, and peaceful

The ocean's deep hues
So pristine gleaming and true
Paradise and peace

A cool breeze passes
Warm sun rays shining all day
Sweet sunsets by night

JOSEPH R. ADOMAVICIA

SECTION 3: TANKA

Safe Spots

Take trips to safe spots

Silence serves as solitude

Take a breath or two

Most troubles clear like rain squalls

in the heat of summer days

Acceptance

Of people you meet
look into their souls so you
accept difference
Difference does not equate
to hate Please open your eyes

<u>Sunset</u>

Cotton candy skies

all this passion in disguise

easing my mind's eye

Vast pinks and blues through and through

Tapestry of happiness

Summertime

Pink flowers blooming

Beauty relishing my life

Tranquility's grasp

curating colors galore

An eloquent arrival

Be Happy

Dew drops form on grass

Fresh air crisp against my face

Morning has arrived

Coffee aroma awaits

Be happy today all day

Faces in the Glass

Fog on the window
Stubby fingers draw a face
Warm breath forms canvas
Memories of us as kids
remain alive through my life

Unlocking the Cage

The key to the cage

It rests in this heart of mine

It will unlock soon

Turning my back to the past

It was much fun I learnt much

In My Head

Like the earth rotates

my mind revolves around thoughts

Wild winded head space

rips through my lone solitude

Silence speaks echoes inside

Our Universe

My spark in the dark

My light while I am in fright

Kindling to my flame

My star within galaxies

Our universe yearns to be

Ease My Senses

Tap fear from my spine

Take weary thoughts from my mind

Draw pain from my heart

Ease the doubt in my fingers

Box my being into her

<u>Know Your Path Too</u>

If you follow suit

you never know what you'll learn

Dare to walk new paths

Just know when to hit the brakes

Don't end up the laughingstock

Be Calm

Take a deep full breath

Exhale inhale slow it down

Don't get so revved up

Red-lining does the heart harm

It wears your gears too early

Sweet Spots

Like vipers phantoms

sift through the frigid night air

Spectral fingertips

crawling just above the skin

Your sweet spots now unsweetened

My Inspiration

You still inspire me

Us and our love together

is all I've wanted

Is this what people call fate

Or have I wandered weary

You Found My Light

Even when I said
that I was not any good
still you found a way
to a modicum of light
in the depths of a cavern

Sanctuary

My fading footsteps

My lone imprints washed away

Embrace the future

finding solace in hardships

A better me I shall be

White Flag

Blood and a white flag

Fatal blow to family

I hope peace is found

Yearly visits won't cut it

A name in stone can't heal pain

Potency

I give and I gave
my love not afraid to lose
inner potency
Match my effort or please leave
I've no time to sip poison

Where is Home Now?

Lonely thoughts can kill

Manic depressive landslides

Who then has your back

Is their love gone now empty

Where will my home reside now

Bittersweet

Pain is too bitter

and sometimes joy is too sweet

Steady rhythmic beat

April fools and trick or treat

Don't fall dragging careless feet

There is an End

As foul as it is
Our country will survive this
It wasn't meant to fall
nor were its people to fret
There is an end to the storm

My Time of the Year

When Autumn's leaves fall
is when my mind has found rest
Watching colors change
reminds me it's not too late
A new year welcoming me

SAKURA

Is It In You?

Riddle me this friend

Does the darkness grab your heart

in the light of day

Have you the gall to resist

Have you the courage to live

It's Our Choices

Harmony broken

Continental wide breakdown

It's now or never

Sever wasteful ideals

Fight as one or die as one

I've Ignited

Our fire in the night

Our tangled tussling bodies

Our lover's delight

Our tangible energy

Our nevers and forevers

G Zero Zero (G00)

Sweat rolls down my face
Another day in the books
G Zero Zero
Running to leave and E-Stop
I forgot my keys inside

(G00 or G Zero Zero is a CNC Machining code
that makes a rapid tool movement)

Memorial Day

Memorial day

Remembrance of the fallen

American pride

Men and women fought boldly

Vigilant and glorified

JOSEPH R. ADOMAVICIA

SECTION 4: CHOKA

Advice From an Old Friend

An old friend told me,

work with your resolve, it stuck.

I learnt to observe

how pristine water glistens.

I learnt to take heed

of the angry thunder's roars.

I learnt to admire

how the tall, lazy palms sway

and how the wind whips.

I learnt how to comprehend

the way our tongues speak

and to not speak too quickly.

I learnt to see through

the dense thickness of the fog;

there is more ahead,

the eye of the storm will pass.

I learnt to adapt

when circumstances stacked high.

Adversity rose;

the ocean's bitter high tide.

I learnt to respect,

that respect is give and take,

like subtle sea tides

weathered through these conditions.

I learnt to focus

JOSEPH R. ADOMAVICIA

lightening-bolt precision,

make actions swiftly;

each decision regret-less.

I learnt to forgive,

for the sea moves without it.

Ocean's grief drowning

or the first breath of fresh air.

I learnt that patience

is more than waiting for peace;

It's being who's brave.

I learnt all my life's presence

is all the resolve in me.

<u>Sakura</u>

Blossoming quickly

An ephemeral life-span

Gone gone with the wind

Pink petals fall with purpose

In a new season is life

Stage Left

I came in stage right,
I stood a while, read poems.
Do they understand?
I recite and speak to say
all that is me and
these poems are more than words,
they have revived me,
they are paramount to life.
Do they understand
haiku, senryu, tanka,
choka, concrete, or
free verse, my rhyme, my iambs,
or cadence like songs?
Do they truly understand?
Times up, I exit stage left.

Author Bio:

Joseph R. Adomavicia

is a 27 year-old resident of Waterbury, Connecticut

that works at Edward Segal Incorporated,

as a CNC Machinist.

He is a published poet,

and has been writing for approximately 5 years.

He is the author of

A Step Into My Heart; Blackout Poetry Edition

and Love Unbound. Mr. Adomavicia's poetry

can also be found in

Z Publishing House's Anthology

of Connecticut's Best Emerging Poets

as well as America's Emerging Poets NE Region.

Photo Credit to Lauren Howard

www.ingramcontent.com/pod-product-compliance
Lightning Source LLC
Chambersburg PA
CBHW051405290426
44108CB00015B/2155